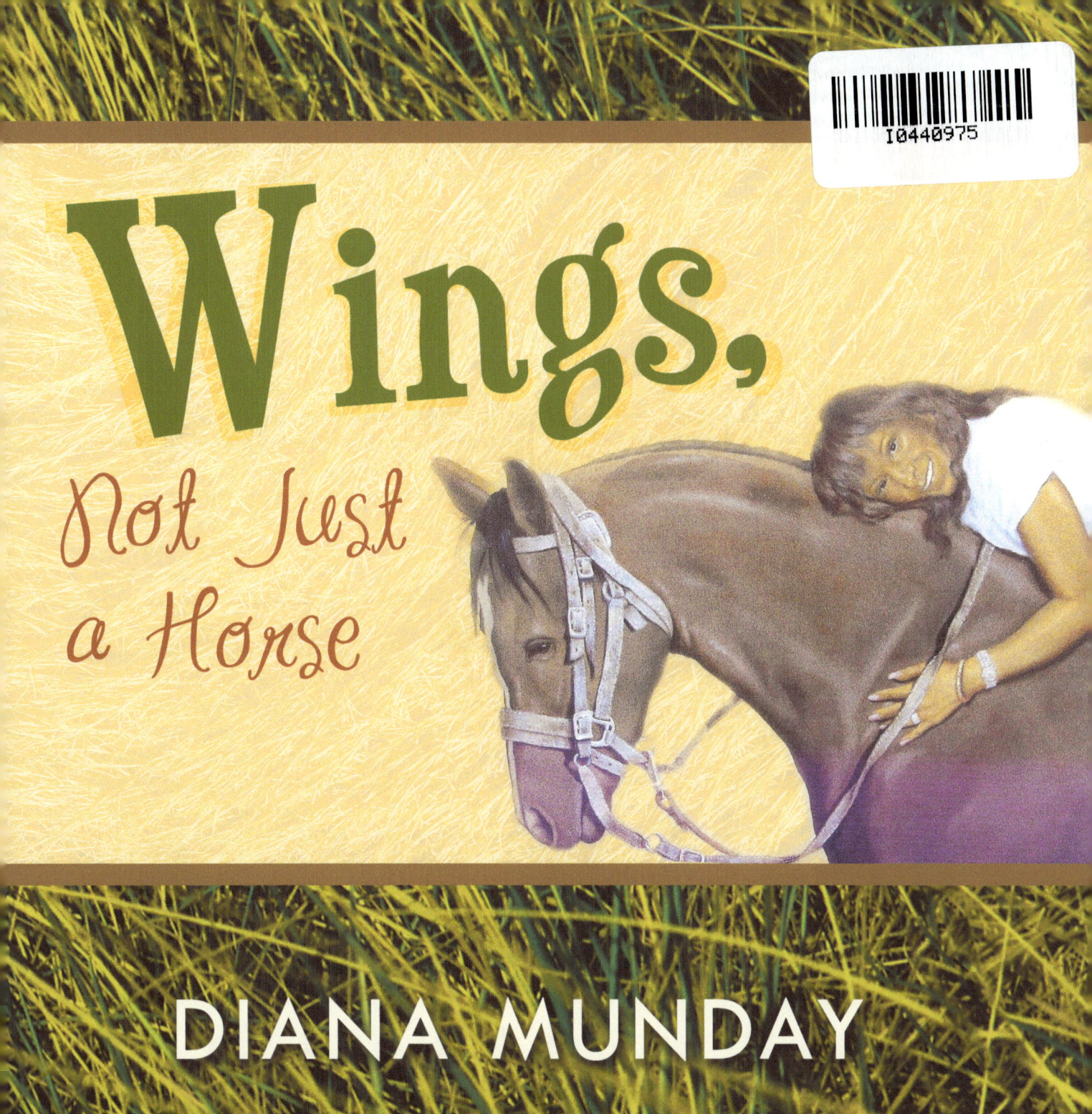

Wings,

Not Just a Horse

DIANA MUNDAY

Order this book online at www.trafford.com
or email orders@trafford.com

Most Trafford titles are also available at major online book retailers.

Printed in the United States of America.

ISBN: 978-1-4269-6524-1

Trafford rev. 04/29/2011

Trafford
PUBLISHING®   www.trafford.com

North America & international
toll-free: 1 888 232 4444 (USA & Canada)
phone: 250 383 6864 ♦ fax: 812 355 4082

Wings,

Not Just a Horse

My name is Diana. I grew up in a typical upper middle class home, the middle of three children. I was rather shy growing up and I have always loved animals, all animals. I always seemed to be able to relate to animals better than I could with people.

As a young girl I had just about every pet you can imagine from chickens, to rodents, to cats, dogs, and even reptiles. It's amazing how many pets I had considering the fact my mother really did not like animals, especially big ones. And she considered anything over the size of a cat too big. Every time I got a pet she said, "This is the last one you can have". But time would go by, and inevitably I would bring home another animal. I would have to listen to moms ranting but it was always worth it. These animals comforted me and I never took on more than I could give my time, love, and attention to.

I always had a knack for treating wounded animals and the neighbors would always bring me injured and abandoned animals. I spent many nights feeding abandoned kittens, birds that had fallen out of nests, cats that had been abused by humans, etc. I loved taking care of these little creatures and felt like it was my calling.

Like most young girls I grew up loving horses. They were the most beautiful and graceful creatures on earth. I remember watching, "My friend Flicka" when I was very young. I loved that movie and I knew one day I would have my own horse. In the years that followed when asked what I wanted for each birthday or Christmas my response was always the same, "A pony". But every birthday and Christmas ended the same, no pony. My mom was scared to death of horses and kept saying they were too expensive and she could not help me take care of it because of her fear for them. My dad was always at work and would not have time to help me either. I eventually gave up asking for a horse by the age of thirteen because I knew it would have to wait until I was old enough to do it on my own.

I remember that as a young teenager whenever I would get mad at my mom I would tell her, "One day I'm going to live in Norco, I'm going to have horses, and you will never want to come over". I really had no idea where Norco was when I was saying it. I was about ten years old when a neighbor told me there was a city called Norco where everyone had horses in their yards. It stuck in my head and I knew one day I would live there and have my horses in my yard.

By the time I was a teenager my Sundays became occupied at a nearby stable where I would rent horses for several hours. I loved riding, and it came easy for me. I was never good at sports but I could ride any horse given to me. I remember my favorite was a small Quarter paint named Spot. I had all the confidence in the world when it came to riding and my balance got better with each and every horse. Years would go by and I would read book after book on care of horses preparing myself for the day I would own my own horse. I babysat almost every day after school and I saved every penny so eventually I could buy my horse.

Within a few months after graduating high school I had a job and this of course this gave me the financial ability to do what I had said I would do for years, own a horse. I started looking at horse ads and checking out stables. I was determined to do this on my own and I had to be prepared for everything.

After searching for horses at a few stables I found a wonderful Quarter horse named Becky. I didn't tell anyone I had bought a horse. I wanted to keep it a secret for a while. Of course I am not sure if my mom caught on since I did come home dusty and smelling like a stable every night. About a month later I got the entire family together one Sunday night by telling them I had a surprise. My sister kept telling my mom I was going to get married. My mom said no way was I getting married, but she had a feeling I had a horse. It couldn't be the fact I smelled like one every day, could it? Once the family was together I loaded them in the car and took them to the stable to introduce them to Becky. Everyone was shocked, except for mom of course. She did not get too close to Becky but at least I got her out of the car.

Becky would teach me everything about horses; caring for them, putting up with my mistakes, and polishing up my riding. I could not have had a better teacher as she was a very patient and forgiving horse.

I met a lot of friends at the stable and they taught me tons more about how to care for Becky. It was from this group of girls that I learned to ride bareback. I was the only one using a saddle and they used to tease me about it. One afternoon we were getting ready to go for a ride and they had taken my saddle from me and hid it. I had no choice but to join them bareback. I loved it and never again used a saddle unless we were trailering out to do serious riding.

Becky was eventually diagnosed with navicular. It is when a small bone down in the hoof rotates. It is common for Quarter horses because of their build, and there is no cure for it. Eventually she would be lame and not rideable. But it takes years to get to that point and I knew we had a lot of good trail rides ahead of us.

A couple of years later I found myself looking for a second horse. I had fallen in love with Arabs. Some of my friends had them and they had the stamina for trail riding because of their size. They are small in stature compared to other breeds. Where other horses have six lumbar vertebrae and eighteen tail bones; the Arab has five lumbar vertebrae and sixteen tail bones. While this makes their backs shorter, it also makes their backs stronger. They have a luxurious long mane and tail, and a dished (concave) face with a tapering muzzle. They are also quite spirited and not recommended for first time horse owners.

In my mind the perfect horse would be an Arab and Quarter cross. I wanted the Arab dished head, with the hind quarters of a Quarter horse. I wanted the intelligence of both breeds, and the stamina of the Arab. I was also going to look for a gelding because it seemed like most mares were too moody. The perfect age would be about 8 years old. Hopefully he would be well broke, good mannered, and love to ride trails.

It was the week before Christmas 1981, a beautiful Saturday afternoon and a perfect day to go horse shopping. My friend, Pam and I hit the road east to Norco with my list of prospects. Yes, I finally found Norco. It is a town in Riverside County, about 30 miles from my home and the stable. We looked at a few horses, and we rode a few horses but I did not find anything I really connected with and it was getting late in the day. I was ready to head home but Pam insisted we had time for one more. She had seen an ad in the local magazine for a 2 year old Arab/Morgan filly. I was not interested in such a young horse, nor did I want a filly, but I was willing to appease Pam with one more horse.

We headed to a property that had about a half dozen horses out front of their home. One horse in particular stood out. She was a beautiful bay Arab filly. She came to the fence to greet us. At the same time the owner was coming out to also greet us and introduce us to Wings, her 2 year old Arab/Morgan filly. Wings had beautiful brown eyes and a narrow blaze down the middle of her face. The Morgan horse showed in her beautiful wide back end which sprouted a tail only a few inches long because of being chewed off by a younger horse.

Wings, age two

I took one long look into Wings' eyes and I knew I had to have her. They were the typical large Arab eyes but they had a kindness to them. There was an instant connection between the two of us. I don't know what I was thinking, I had never broken a horse before and I was hoping to get one older and ready for the trail. But Pam reassured me she would help me break her. Wings was gorgeous and sweet and I had to have her.

Wings came home on Christmas Eve day. I considered her my Christmas present to myself that year. I was able to put her into a stall next to Becky at the stable. I would need Becky to help me train my new filly the same way she had trained me. Wings had only had a halter on her at this point and we were going to have a long road ahead of us to get her ready for riding by age four.

As the days and weeks passed I realized how easy Wings was to train. She had a lot of energy as Arabs are known for, especially young ones. She is by far the most affectionate horse I have ever been around. By affectionate I mean she is always at my shoulder, sometimes resting her large head on my shoulder. There are instances when she may not be feeling so well and she will give you a horse hug, holding you between her large head and her neck. Sometimes it can be painful when she holds you too tightly.

By far, the most embarrassing thing about Wings is the fact she likes to have her udders rubbed. She will stand in front of you and lift her hind leg not letting you go by until you rub her. This can be quite intimidating when someone is not used to being around horses. Some people would think she was trying to kick them until I tell them they need to put their hand under her belly and scratch her.

Wings is more than willing to try anything I ask her to do, no matter how silly it was. And young girls can come up with a lot of silly things to do with horses. One of our favorites was, "Fire in the barn". We would place blindfolds over their eyes and see how long they would let us lead them or even ride them. We did not keep blindfolds in our tack sheds so we would cover their eyes with our sweaters, rags, or anything else we could find that was long enough to go around their faces. I am sure this idea came from watching one too many western movies.

One thing I never tired of was watching Wings run loose in the arena. Arabs run with their tails straight up in the air, and their nostrils flared. They are so light on their feet it almost looks like they have springs on their hooves as they float across the ground. It is the most beautiful sight in the world to watch the gracefulness of such a big animal.

Most of the first year for Wings would be spent following me and Becky out on trail. Wings did not need a halter and lead line to follow us. She would follow Becky the same way any young horse would follow behind their mother. Becky was patient putting up with a rambunctious 3 year old running around her, bumping her, and occasionally trying to nurse from her. Wings was not good about staying right at my side as she would rather take advantage of stopping to eat weeds growing along the trail. I did not worry about her because I knew she would never get far enough behind to let us out of her sight. And if I felt she was taking too long snacking all I had to do was call her and she would come running to me.

Soon she would be turning 4 years old. This is the age I had decided would be good to start riding her. Her tail had grown out and was about half way to the ground. By now I had her on a lead line when we would go out on trail. She needed to listen to my voice commands to Becky so she could learn them. I had started putting different bits in her mouth. She was getting saddles on her back and getting used to the cinch getting tightened up around her belly. Like most horses she kicks at her belly when I would cinch the saddle up. Of course the kick was always associated with a nasty look back to me. I ignored her nasty look. I had already learned she would never actually hurt me.

One day I had her loose in the arena as I sat on the fence watching her run. All of a sudden I had an overwhelming desire to sit on her. I had been waiting for so long to get on her back, and I was only 2 months away from the magical, "Age 4". She must have read my mind because she came to the fence and put herself close enough to the fence for me to slide on. I did not know what to expect, maybe I would get bucked, maybe she would rear, or maybe she would take off in a dead run and I would just fall off. I knew anything was possible but for some reason I did not feel fear. I only felt the anxiety to be on her, to finally be a part of her. I slid on and waited. But she just stood there. I said, "Walk" and that is exactly what she did, ever so carefully, she just walked. She took my command and did exactly what was expected of her as if she had been doing it for years. When I got off I ran to find Pam and let her know what had just happened. We agreed, it's time to start riding my Arab filly.

A few weeks went by and I was riding Wings around the stable. Although she has been out on trail by lead line with Becky I had not ridden her out of the stable yet. Pam was one of the girls who had taught me to ride bareback years before. Because none of us girls rode with saddles all of our horses were trained to line up with a fence, a rock, whatever was around to help us get on. They were also trained that we can get on from the right or the left. You never know when you will be out on the trail and have a cliff on one side.

One day I asked Pam to come help me with teaching Wings to "Fence". Our usual training consisted of the rider on the fence with reins in hand. The trainee horse in the middle and the experienced horse on the outside forcing the trainee in the middle close to the fence for the rider to get on. It usually takes a couple of lessons for the trainee to figure out how to line up with a fence whenever the rider approaches one with the reins in hand. Wings had it figured out before Pam even got there. From afar Pam watched as I went to a fence near Wings' stall. As soon as I approached the fence Wings lined up and put her back close to the fence. She got as close as she could without hurting me in between. By now Pam was close to me and we were trying to figure out how Wings knew what to do. We figured she must have learned by watching Becky do it hundreds of times before her. This will not be the last time Wings seems to learn something by watching.

On a few occasions I would ride Becky and/or Wings to my home. My home was only about 2 miles from the stable and I could be there in about 30 minutes. I had a young neighbor girl who liked to go riding and she would ride Becky for me. The signal to the neighborhood kids that Diana is home with the horses was my mothers high pitched screaming. It is hard to describe the actual deafening sound my mother made but you could faintly make out her telling me to, "Get away from the house with my crazy animals". It is a sound that is embedded in my mind for life. My mom would actually run from door to door locking all the exterior doors to the house as she screamed. She would even close the curtains on the sliding glass doors so the horses would not run through them to come in the house. I don't think she realized that my horses, as smart as they were, were never trained to open doors. In fact, I don't remember them ever trying to go into a house. You just had to laugh at mom.

While at home I would give the neighbor children horse rides out on my front lawn. When everyone had a ride I would go back to the stable. At this point my mom got to open the curtains and doors. Now, almost 30 years later, those kids are grown up with kids of their own. They love to talk to their children about the days I would bring home my horses and give them all rides. It's great to know I made such fond memories for them.

Some friends were going to go camping with their horses for the weekend to Coto de Caza. Coto was a beautiful hunt club which consisted of thousands of acres of untouched nature. There is a stable on the property, a small malt shop/small grocery store, and one small area of about 30 custom homes for some of the club members. I had been invited by friends to go for the weekend. I jumped at the invitation. This would be Wings' first outing and I was dying to see how she would do.

We all arrived to Coto without any problems. There were probably about a dozen riders. We got all of the horses out of their trailers and tied off to the outside of the trailers where they would be spending the next two days. It was a beautiful sunny day and the group of us wanted to take a walk around to enjoy the serenity and beauty of it all. Of course the best way to soak in all this beauty is with a malt. We were out for about an hour when we got to the malt shop. I was sitting outside the store with another friend, Sarah. In the distance we could hear a horse whinny. A few seconds later we heard it again and this time the whinny sounded familiar. Sarah and I looked at each other in disbelief as we both turned to see where the whinny was coming from. At the top of a hill, probably a half mile in the distance stood my Arab, Wings. She came running down the hill dragging her lead line and talking to me the whole way down. Now there are two things you have to understand with this scenario. First, when we left the trailers we headed north and now we were east of our campsite. How did she know to come east? Was it luck, a good guess, instinct, or had she been running around for an hour looking for me? Second, horses are herd animals and they don't leave their herd. I know I was told Arabs are real people horses, but this was ridiculous, and almost embarrassing. My horse had untied herself from the trailer, left the other horses to come look for me in a place neither she nor I had ever been to. This is just the beginning of her showing me what a special horse she is and what a special bond was being created between me and my Wings. Thankfully the rest of the weekend was pretty uneventful and Wings was great for her first time out on trail.

Wings on her first trail ride to Coto

Just like learning how much Arabs are true people horses I will also learn from Wings how instinct comes into play when it involves children. Sarah had a young son named Steven. One particular day there was a group of us out on a trail ride. I was near the rear of the group and Sarah and Steven were in front, each on their own horse. In the distance I could hear Steven cry but did not think anything of it. I could see he was still on his horse and near his mother. I continued talking to a friend when all of a sudden Wings bolted into a run. I could not stop her and I did not know the reason for it at that point. I only knew I had better hang on. She found Steven and went to him, putting her large face into his lap almost as if to say, "I am here now and everything will be ok". No one in the group could believe what they had witnessed. Never before had anyone seen a horse feel so compelled to comfort a child. Steven would play cry several times over the next few years always to get Wings to run to his side. Sometimes I was on her back and sometimes she was loose in the stable. Wherever she was, she always seemed to hear his cry and would run to his side time and time again.

On another occasion I had been out camping for the weekend with Sarah, Steven, and Sarah's husband, Tom. It was very late Sunday night when we arrived back to the stable and we had a few horses to unload before the night was over. Wings was in the front of the trailer which meant she would be unloaded last. We were not allowed to drive the horse trailers into the stable which meant a long hike to take Sarah's horses to their stalls at the very last row of stalls, hike back up to the front of the stable to get Wings, and head back down again to put her away. Sarah and I quickly got her 2 horses unloaded, to their stalls, and put to bed. We quickly headed back to the trailer to find it empty. We asked Tom where Wings was. He told us he put Steven on her and sent him to put her away. Now remember, Wings has just really started to be ridden, she is full of energy, Steven had nothing but a halter on her, and the fact that Sarah and I did not come across them on our way back to the trailer set our minds adrift. At this point panic sets in and the vision of Wings bolting, leaving an injured Steven in the dirt is filling our minds as we dart back into the stable screaming Stevens name. Both of us side by side shouting his name, looking down expecting to find a half conscious child clinging for his life, and a half crazed Arab running loose in the stable. Finally we heard Steven, "Mom, I'm here at Wings' stall".

9

Sitting calmly on her back waiting for someone to remove him was a very safe Steven. He wanted to know what was wrong with us. Two crazed women running to him as if we were surprised to see him alive. He laughed and said she just walked very slowly back to her stall on her own. Sarah removed Steven, I removed the halter, and put Wings to bed. But not before kissing her and telling her I was sorry for not giving her the benefit of the doubt knowing she was carrying her precious cargo.

One of the girls I loved to go riding with was Natalie and her horse, Cider. But it seemed like every time I went with Natalie we ended up with a catastrophe. Perhaps we were forgetting we were not immortal and got into the habit of doing things not so safe or smart. On one occasion we had trailered out and went swimming in the Santa Ana River. I did not feel anything unusual, but when we got out of the water Wings was bleeding excessively from the inside of her rear left leg. When I finally found the source of the blood I found three puncture marks on the inside of her upper leg. It looked like a piece of metal rebar had gone through her leg. I called the vet from the river and told him I would meet him at the stable in thirty minutes. I felt very bad knowing I was the one that asked her to go into the water. I wanted to feel the sensation of riding a horse while it was swimming. Another idea I got from watching too many cowboys cross the Rio Grande. A visit with the vet and a week of rest and Wings was feeling pretty good again. I never again went to that area to go swimming.

On another trip with Natalie we ended up in quicksand. Not quicksand like you would see in a movie where they sink to the middle of the earth, but California river quicksand. The difference is river quicksand is not as deep. You cannot get out without assistance, but at least you know you're not going to die. Like movie quicksand it is wet, really wet, and really messy. Natalie and I started out on a ride near the river when we came across a rider who warned us that the river had changed course and to stay only on trails where we saw hoof prints and knew riders had gone before us. We said thank you, but we were experienced riders and we knew what we were doing so we went on our merry way knowing we were going into forbidden territory.

It was not 30 minutes before we ran into trouble and walked right into river quicksand. Wings and Cider were side by side. I think Wings hit it first, but when Cider hit the sand she reared and was able to turn and keep her and Natalie safely out of it. It was too late for me and Wings. We were in it, and when we hit it Wings went down. I came off her back and ended up next to her. Legs flailing everywhere, mine more than Wings'. Luckily we always ride with halters over the bridles and carry our lead lines with us. This made it possible for Natalie to throw us a lead line. I was able to get it attached to Wings' halter and Cider backed up and dragged her out of the wet, sandy mess. Yes, just like in the movies. Now it was my turn. Natalie threw the line back to me and pulled me out on my belly. Imagine going to the beach and going into the water fully dressed, now come out and roll around in the sand from head to toe. That's what we looked like. Sand was in my hair, in my boots; my saddle was covered in it. As embarrassing it was I was glad to just be out of it. What seemed like an hour as my life passed before me was probably just about five minutes. Never again would I go out on a trail where I did not see hoof prints.

By now Wings and I were going out for weekend camping about 2-3 times a month. I would go anywhere, and with anyone who asked. Sometimes we stayed the night, and sometimes we just made a day of it. The more I rode my Arab the more I fell in love with her. She was sure footed, she never tired, and she would do anything asked of her. On trail rides she insisted on being in front. She loved to find the deer trails and every one of my friends was used to letting her lead. I literally dropped my reins and let her go wherever she wanted. She had always gotten us home safe and I had started to trust her with my life. When we got tired we would give her the command, "Go home". In the hundreds of trail rides she would never turn around to go home, but find another trail and get us back to our trailers. She usually had us back within 30 minutes no matter where we were. All my friends were amazed at her instinct and understanding of the command. My friends have also gotten used to the fact that we knew we will always end up lost. No matter how many times we may have repeated a campground or a trail we undoubtedly would end up lost and end our day telling Wings to get us home.

On one camping trip Pam and I were to meet Sarah and Tom at a new equestrian campground close to Temecula. Sarah and Tom left early in the day but Pam and I had to work so we left a little later that day. We had directions, but just like in riding we ended up lost. We got off the freeway, headed down a dirt road and when we felt we were going in the wrong direction we tried to turn around and got stuck in sand. There we were lost again, no vehicle, and it was starting to get dark. You are probably reading this and wondering why we didn't use our cell phone and call someone for help. I wish it was that easy, but this was 1984 and cell phones had not been invented yet. We had one mode of transportation left available to us and that was our horses. We unloaded the horses and hopped on their backs with only a halter. I told Pam I wanted to let Wings go and see where she would take us. After all, she always got us home. Could she understand me telling her to get us to the campsite? Pam wanted to backtrack and see where we missed our turn. I jumped on Wings with only a halter and I told her to look for her boyfriend Troy, Tom's horse. I told her several times to go to Troy, find Troy.

Pam took off back down the dirt road on April. Wings and I took off deep into a dark forest of trees. There I was, trusting my horse to once again get me to where I needed to be. I don't remember being too scared and I know I should have been. Here I was just me and my horse, nothing but a halter, it's getting dark, and I am out in the middle of nowhere. Less than 5 minutes into our adventure I could hear Pam and April approaching from behind us. All Pam said was, "I trust Wings more than April". And off we went deeper into the thick cluster of trees. It took her about 20 minutes, but she did it. As we approached the campsite she gave a big whinny and announced our arrival. Again you have to think; was it luck, was it instinct, or did she understand my command to find Troy? Whatever it was, she got us to the campsite. Everyone came out and asked why we were coming in from the trees, and on horseback. Where was the trailer? Pam and I told everyone what had happened. Tom grabbed his truck and found where we left our truck and trailer. He hooked up a chain and with ease got us out of the sand. We followed him back to the campsite. It was a wonderful weekend after that with great riding, great friends, and of course the greatest horse ever.

A few times a year the stable would have play days. We would do silly games such as playing polo with brooms, racing with eggs on spoons, basically relay races on horseback. They were fun days, and some of the best memories I have. By now Wings was an old pro at riding, and she could pick up any game at the drop of a hat.

One game was for all the riders to remove their shoes and put them in a pile at the far end of an arena. The riders line up on horseback, gallop to the pile of shoes, dismount, find their shoes, jump back on their horse, and the first one back wins. I would barely have one shoe on and in a stirrup when Wings would be in a dead run back to the starting point as I put on my second shoe. Yes, we would win, over and over again. She seemed to know what to do without being asked. I never had reins in my hands; I was putting on the second shoe. All I had to say was, "Go". She only had to know I was ready for the ride back.

Another game was keyhole. The horse has to run thru a small opening which turns into a circle. They have to spin in a 360 and come back out the same opening without stepping on the line. It is a timed event and done in a full run.

Picture an actual keyhole with a very narrow opening. Some of the horses were very good at this since it is an actual event with gymkhana horses. Wings has never done gymkhana but I let her watch from the sidelines. Remember, she learns by watching. After being pressured by my friends I decided to try it. I knew if she was paying attention she would not need much guidance from me. I just had to hold on and let her do her thing. We got to the gate and I gave her the word she loved, "Go"! She took off in a dead run, thru the hole, spun, and back out again. I never took the reins. I let her do it and she did not let me down. She did it without error and came in second to a gymkhana horse, Cider. I was so proud of her. She loved the games and always came home with ribbons.

In 1984 I had decided to quit my job and go to college on a full time basis. I planned to work weekends to earn money to support me and my horses. Becky was getting older, the navicular was getting worse, and I was riding Wings more than her. I had decided to turn her out in a pasture in Diamond Bar. It was a beautiful area, over 100 acres, and only about 30 minutes from home. I could have her out there, visit her on weekends, and ride until my heart was content. It was a hard decision to make. I was so used to her being just two miles from home where I visited her and Wings every single day. But putting her out in Diamond Bar would help me out with my time and money being more restricted. Pam also loved the idea of trailering April up there to ride with us on weekends.

Pam and I took Becky up to Diamond Bar on a Sunday afternoon. I unloaded her from the trailer and walked her to an open grassy area. It was hard for me to walk away from her. I had this feeling in my gut that it was going to be the last time I would see her. I had to tell myself I was just imagining it, and I left her. This would end up being the biggest mistake of my life.

The following Saturday Pam and I went up to visit and ride Becky. But I could not find her anywhere. She was not with the herd of horses down in the valley. And after several hours of looking for her we realized she was no where on the property. My gut feeling had been correct. Our only conclusion was someone had stolen her. I had a police report taken but I would never see Becky again and we would never know what really happened out there. My heart was broken and years later to hear her name would bring tears to my eyes. She will forever hold a special place in my heart.

This is the last time I ever saw Becky

Time would go by and Wings and I would go on rides every day, rain or shine. It didn't matter what the weather was, we just rode. If it was raining I had an umbrella. If it was hot out the girls were in shorts, bathing suit tops, and barefoot. We continued to come up with more riding games. One really dumb game was done while we were all in a gallop. One rider would approach another horse and rider, removing their bridle. This meant the rider was helpless. Their horse would run with the rest of the horses and all the rider could do was hold on until we stopped. I do not recommend this game for anyone, and I would kill my sons if they ever came home and told me they had played this themselves. But we thought we were immortal at that age. We were full of life, and we were stupid.

More years would go by and I got engaged to be married. We bought a home in Chino Hills, just west of Norco, the city I always threatened my mother with. Wings will have to be stabled out there. My days of camping would be far and few between since I was leaving the stable with all my friends, their trailers, and Wings' friends.

The great thing about the new stable is lots of riding trails close by. They also have play days at the new stable. More relay races on horseback! They also had horse shows. I had never competed in shows, but I was sure Wings would be up to new challenges.

After watching a few shows I decided to take western riding lessons. I was used to trail riding, and there are a few things Wings will have to learn to do, like holding her head just right and picking up the correct lead while in a gallop. A few lessons into it and I was sure we were both ready for our first show. I bought new silver tack for Wings and show clothes for me. She was almost a completely different horse in the arena. No matter how any other horse acted up she concentrated on me only, never noticing a run away horse or screaming people outside the arena. I loved showing with her and there was not a day she did not bring home ribbons. The more she showed the better she got. Ribbons went from third place, to second place, and eventually to first place. There was one particular event, "Bareback riding" that we remained undefeated in, in the years of showing. Each show I had people come up and mock me, telling me we were going to loose our title to them. But we never did. Wings and I retired showing with our title in tact. Thank you to Pam and Natalie for hiding my saddle and forcing me to learn to ride bareback. Eventually I got older and I let the younger girls show.

Wings and I just
before a show

In June of 1990 I gave birth to my first son, Michael. I would take him to the stable with me. I would put him in a play pen beside me when he was an infant. And as he got older and could sit up he would ride in front of me on Wings. Because he was around horses he had no fear of them. And because he had been around Wings he grew up accustomed to being able to pull on her tail, walk under her stomach, sit under her, and many other things I would never recommend anyone to do with a horse they did not know well. Even if you did know them well you may not be allowed to pull a tail or sit under them safely. But Wings was different and she knew it was her job to protect him and comfort him when needed the same way she did with Steven. She played with Michael with a gentleness I cannot explain. She followed him like a little puppy just inches behind him without any lead line or halter. On a few occasions I would find him playing in the dirt under her belly, Wings not moving a bit.

Of course by the age of 3 Michael wanted his own horse. For his birthday I asked what he wanted and I got a very familiar response, "A pony". And that is exactly what he got, a pony. A small Shetland pony named Strawberry. As small as Strawberry was she has no problem keeping up with me and Wings. She was the perfect size and temperament for Michael.

By now we were paying board for 2 horses at a stable and it was getting expensive. The family was growing and it was time to make a move to a bigger house where we could keep horses on our own property. Yes, you can guess where we ended up. I finally achieved the dream of living in Norco with Wings and Strawberry out my back door. The house my mom would dread because there are horses in my backyard and the only way to visit her grandson was to put up with those huge animals with their big scary eyes.

It is in Norco I gave birth to my second son, Ethan. As much as my boys loved their Strawberry they also loved to play with Wings. The boys came up with some unusual things to teach Wings to do. One of the things Ethan taught Wings was to approach a fence and put her head over the fence. As she had her head over the fence he would have access to her neck. And once on her neck he could slide down to her back. And if they weren't sliding down her neck to her back they were hanging off her neck as she walked around the yard.

Strawberry was getting older and because of complications with scarring on her esophagus we had to put her down. My husband Guy and I told the boys she had to go to the hospital because she was very sick, and she was so sick she could not come home. She was a great starter pony for the boys and both of them will have fond memories of her for their lifetime.

Ethan and Strawberry

It's time to shop for a new pony and a perfect time to get a larger pony since the boys were growing. I had come across my dream pony here in Norco. I went into the yard where she was eating and right away threw my jacket over her head. She barely noticed, but did not spook the way most horses would. I crawled under her belly, I pulled her tail, and I got no response back from her. She was passing all the tests with flying colors. The last test would be to take her on a ride. So I threw a halter on her and took off into the dark. I rode for almost an hour and by the time I got back I knew I wanted her.

This was the pony that I had fantasized about all of my life. She was pure black, long flowing mane, and a tail that would drag on the ground. Her only white was a star on her face. In my fantasy her name was supposed to be Star, but the boys wanted to call her Blackie, so Blackie it was.

She was great with the boys. The boys were small enough and Blackie was big enough that they could both ride her at the same time. It was not unusual to find the boys sitting on her while she ate. They would jump on her and just sit on her while she would walk around the yard. .

Every Easter I would invite family, extended family, and friends over for a huge luncheon. I had a great yard to do Easter egg hunts and everyone would bring eggs to hide and a dish for lunch. On one of those occasions I think my mother must have mixed her medications or there was something in the water because we actually got her to agree to sit on Blackie. Of course as soon as she was up on Blackie the old familiar screaming started. I know she was saying things to me during her screaming. And I can only guess they were things I should not write or repeat. But we got her up on a horse, okay a pony. But this is more than anyone ever thought we would ever do with her. When Guy went to get her down I remember my mother almost strangling him. She had her arms around his neck but she would not release her legs from around Blackie or let go of the saddle horn. It took me and my aunt to pry her legs off of Blackie as she hung on to Guy for dear life. I do remember a crowd of about 50 people crying because they were laughing so hard, my dad included. My dad ended up getting hit from my mom when she got down. She was screaming at him for not getting her down sooner and for laughing at her. We did get pictures. But I wish I had a video for the full audio effect of the event.

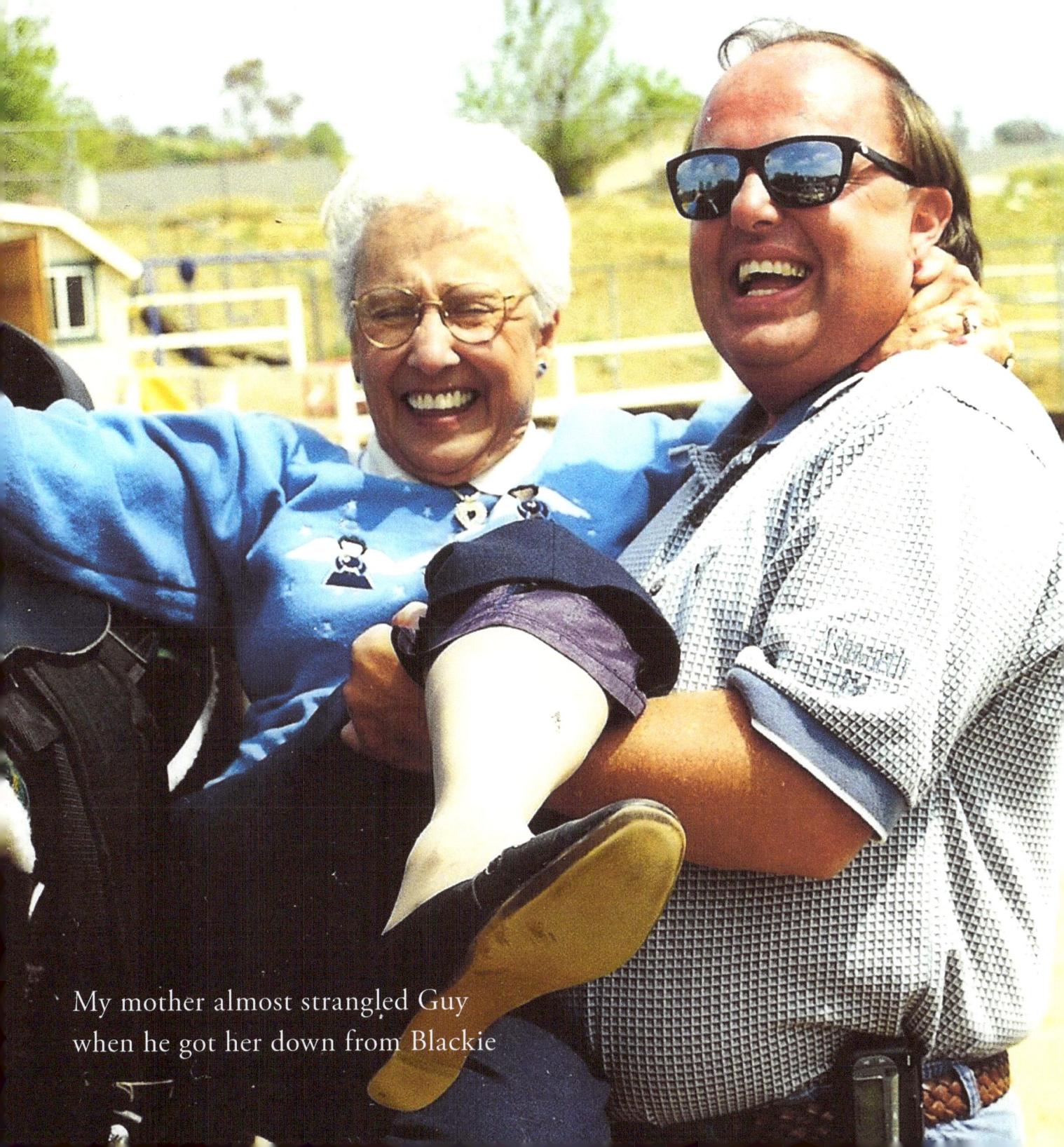

My mother almost strangled Guy
when he got her down from Blackie

My mother died a few months later of a massive heart attack. I always remember something she said when I had first gotten Wings. One of our neighbors was over and said to my mom, "I think Diana loves that horse more than she loves you". My moms response was, "If I can come second to that horse I feel pretty damn special". Not a day, not an hour goes bye that I don't think of my mom. She was a great friend and I miss her daily phone call to check up on me and my boys.

During these years I discovered adult men came up with dumber games than young girls do. We had a set of friends that would come over, Cathy and Stu. Stu was as competitive as Guy, if not more so. One day we were sitting and talking when all of a sudden the men decided to have a competition of horse butt jumping. Yes, one more idea taken from western movies. The object was to have my poor Wings stand in the middle of the yard. Each of them would come running up from behind her. They would put their hands on her butt and lunge themselves forward onto her back. I don't even know why I agreed to such a game, but I did. Stu is tall and built like an athlete, but Guy is short and stout and I was not sure he would get the height needed to propel himself onto her butt. But off I went, Wings in tow. I dropped the lead line and stepped to the side. Stu went first and completed the task with little effort. Now it was Guys turn. He walked about 20 feet behind Wings, jumped in the air a few times as a warm up, now he is ready. Guy was running at full speed in a pair of thongs and nylon shorts. He manages to spring himself onto her butt and then propel himself forward onto her newly brushed back. The back I also sprayed a silicone based cleaner called Show Sheen on. Guy is ecstatic he made it and while his body is still in motion he throws his hands into the air while saying, "Ta Da". At the same time his nylon shorts are reacting with the silicone making it impossible for him to stay up on her back. Stu had to run and catch him before he slid under Wings. Cathy and I were crouched over laughing and wishing we had a camera. No kidding, I had to change my underwear after this event because we were laughing so hard. Wings would have to do this game a few more times on different occasions with different cowboy wannabe's.

The boys were now old enough to take camping with the horses. We only had the two horses so it meant we have to ride double. Wings loved to go in the trailer like a dog likes to go bye-bye. She knew that when I got her trailer leg wraps out of the tack shed she was going to go in the trailer. She would whinny and stand still as I would wrap her legs. You could not get the wraps on fast enough for her.

Most horses you would take by the halter and lead them into the trailer, but not Wings. All I would do is untie her from the stall rail and she would load herself. Guy always thought this was funny and with each trip started to park the trailer further and further away from her. At first the trailer was only 50 feet or so from her. Then he started parking it out of sight in the driveway. While we are camping he liked to actually drive the trailer and hide it. He made Wings look for the trailer so she could load. But it didn't matter because within seconds she could locate her trailer and load herself. Blackie still needed assistance.

During one of our camping trips with the horses we had decided to take one last ride before packing up. I was riding double with Ethan on Blackie and had found a cut off wood post for us to mount from. Guy and Michael went to the same post to mount. Michael was on, and now it was Guys turn to mount. He had just started to put one leg over Wings when all of a sudden he jumped down. He took off running down the dirt road arms waving in the air and screaming much like my mother used to. He had removed his shirt, and as he was about to remove his shorts when I finally caught up to him. It turned out the post was the home to a nest of yellow jackets. As the first three of us stood on the post to mount it was just enough to make them angry and attack the next person which just happened to be Guy. I finally got him to calm down and stop removing his clothes in public. There were no more hornets on Guy, but he had been stung several times. As we went back to our mounting post we found Michael still sitting there on Wings waiting for someone to go riding with him. Luckily neither Michael nor Wings got stung.

Friends of ours wanted to breed their grey Arab stallion to Blackie. I allowed it to happen since I wanted to get a black half Arab baby colt out of Blackie. But Blackie had another idea and she gave birth to a beautiful black filly a year later. The black was only temporary, as you could see the grey undercoat that would shed out and lighten as she aged. I let the boys name her, and of course they came up with none other than, Star.

Blackie was not the smartest pony I have ever encountered. She was great for the kids because of her easy going personality and the fact that she would follow Wings anywhere. She did not like to use her brain too much and that was okay when we were riding with the boys. There was also nothing that bothered her such as loud noises or loose dogs. I knew I was going to have to count on Wings when it came to training the filly, just as Becky helped me train her years before.

Michael resting on Blackie

Star was only a few weeks old when she decided she was not going to be as easy and willing to train as Wings. On one occasion I had gone out back to brush everyone. As I approached Star she took off running and she kept running from me every time I got near her. After about 20 minutes of chasing her I was frustrated, really frustrated and I turned to Wings and in a very loud voice said, "Do you think you can help"? Within seconds Wings had Star cornered in her stall. When Star would try to back up Wings would bite her on her butt and move her forward again. If Star tried to move too far forward Wings would put herself in the way, forcing her to stay in the corner. This made it very easy for me to halter Star. Again, you have to ask, did she understand me or was this a coincidence? I was sure I would have the opportunity to try it again.

As luck would have it Star tried the same game again the very next day. But instead of chasing her for 20 minutes I called to Wings after only a few minutes. Again, Wings came over and cornered Star the very same way she had done the day before. By now I was convinced this is not a coincidence. Whether she understood what I was saying to her, or whether she is helping out because she could sense my frustration. She was there for me, and she did exactly what I needed her to do. You may ask where Blackie was while all of this was going on. Blackie just stood in her stall watching all of it and waiting for her turn to be groomed. Oblivious and not caring about the stress her filly was putting me through.

It was a beautiful Friday night in September. I had a work function to go to and I was going to be late to feed dinner to the animals. Guy also was going to be late but would take care of feeding the horses when he got in. Wings was locked in her stall and very upset that her dinner was late. This was not unusual for her to be angry, but she would usually do something like break a waterline so we would come home to a lake in the yard. What happened next was a freak accident, unpredicted, and it would change her future forever. As Guy approached the yard Wings could see him and knew soon she would get the dinner she had been waiting for. He was only a few yards from her stall when he saw Wings put one foot through the bottom of her gate and get her hoof wedged between the door and the bottom where a wood panel ran across to keep shavings in. As she went to pull it out she got the second front hoof stuck. Guy could see what is going on and went running to Wings' stall. He rushed to her and was able to release her legs from being pinned in the front gate. As he did this she fell back and pulled muscles in her hind leg. Guy immediately began to check how much damage she had done to herself. Not finding much blood he thought she was okay. He said it was one of those moments in life that feels like it was running in slow motion but in actual time you knew it was only a few seconds.

I came home about a half hour later. Guy told me what had happened and I immediately ran out to check her. Besides a couple of small cuts I could tell she had hurt her hind end. But it was not until the vet came out to check her that we realized the extent of the damage. She had pulled a muscle in her hind end causing her to walk with a shorter stride on her right side. You could actually see the protrusion of the muscle from the outside. There was nothing the vet could do for her at her age. At the time he had told me to give her rest and hope she would correct herself to be ridden again. But as months would turn into years she would never get over this injury. My rides we limited to sort jaunts in the backyard. The horse that used to love to go on trail rides would never again leave my yard.

Because of this injury there will be a few occasions where Wings will be laying down on the ground, but unable to get up on her own. When we see this we run out back and flip her to her strong side and help her up.

On one very hot sunny day I was home and happened to look out back only to find Wings lying in the middle of the yard. I went out to her and because of the amount of sweat on her I could tell she had been down for a while. She was already on her stronger side so I put a halter on her to help her get up. As small as I am I was not helpful to her at all. So I hollered to my neighbor and she ran over. Between the two of us we did not budge her at all. When I looked in Wings' eyes I saw something I had never seen before in her life. I could see she had given up. I ran in the house and called my vet. His receptionist, Jen told me Dr. V was on his way. I was crying and my next phone call was to Guy. I did not say anything to Guy except, "Come home now, I need you". Something told him to call Jen and ask if there was something going on with Wings. She told him yes, and he should probably get home.

When I got back out to Wings a sense of panic came over me. Her head was on the ground and her eyes were barely open. I was still crying and I screamed, "Don't you dare leave me today". She opened her eyes, lifted her head, and without any help from me or the neighbor she stood up. She was so proud she was able to get up she started nickering to me. I just kept hugging her and telling her how much I loved her. She would continue nickering for a few more times. At this moment Dr. V came driving in the yard. Guy was pulling up right behind him. Everyone was happy to see she was able to get up. Dr. V examined her and told me she was okay for now. We would just have to watch her. After the Dr. left the neighbor told me she saw the same look of defeat in Wings' eyes that I had seen. But she did not want to mention it to me for fear of upsetting me more than I already was.

On January 12, 2009 Wings turned 30 years old. I had been saying for years if Wings made it to 30 we were going to have a huge party for her, and I kept my word. Months before her party my son, Michael and I started painting a western town backdrop. It consisted of 5 sheets of plywood that were painted like the front of a western town. It included the jail, the bank, the stable, the hotel, and the grocery store. We had a lot of fun painting it. I had also started buying western things online such as western bath towels, wanted posters, horse lights, and I special ordered the game, "Pin the tail on Wings". My plan was to eat on pie tins like you would see in movies around the campfire. The tables were decorated with ceramic boots, western scarves, and baskets of carrots. Her birthday cake was none other than a carrot cake. The invitations were handmade with a hand drawn picture of Wings on the front. These went out to 120 of my closest friends. It was wonderful to have so many people show up for a horse's birthday party. The day was like a wedding, months of planning and then over in just a few hours.

Wings is still in my yard and she still knickers at mealtimes and when she sees the boys come home. Her pellets have to be softened since she only has a few teeth left. Many of them have fallen out over the years, maybe due to age, maybe due to all the Starbursts and Skittles candy she likes to eat. I don't like to leave her alone for more than a few hours at a time for fear she will lay down and not be able to get up.

She is 32 years old now. I consider every day I have with her a gift. She has been much more than just a horse to me. She has been my best friend and companion for 30 years, and I am thankful for having her in my life..

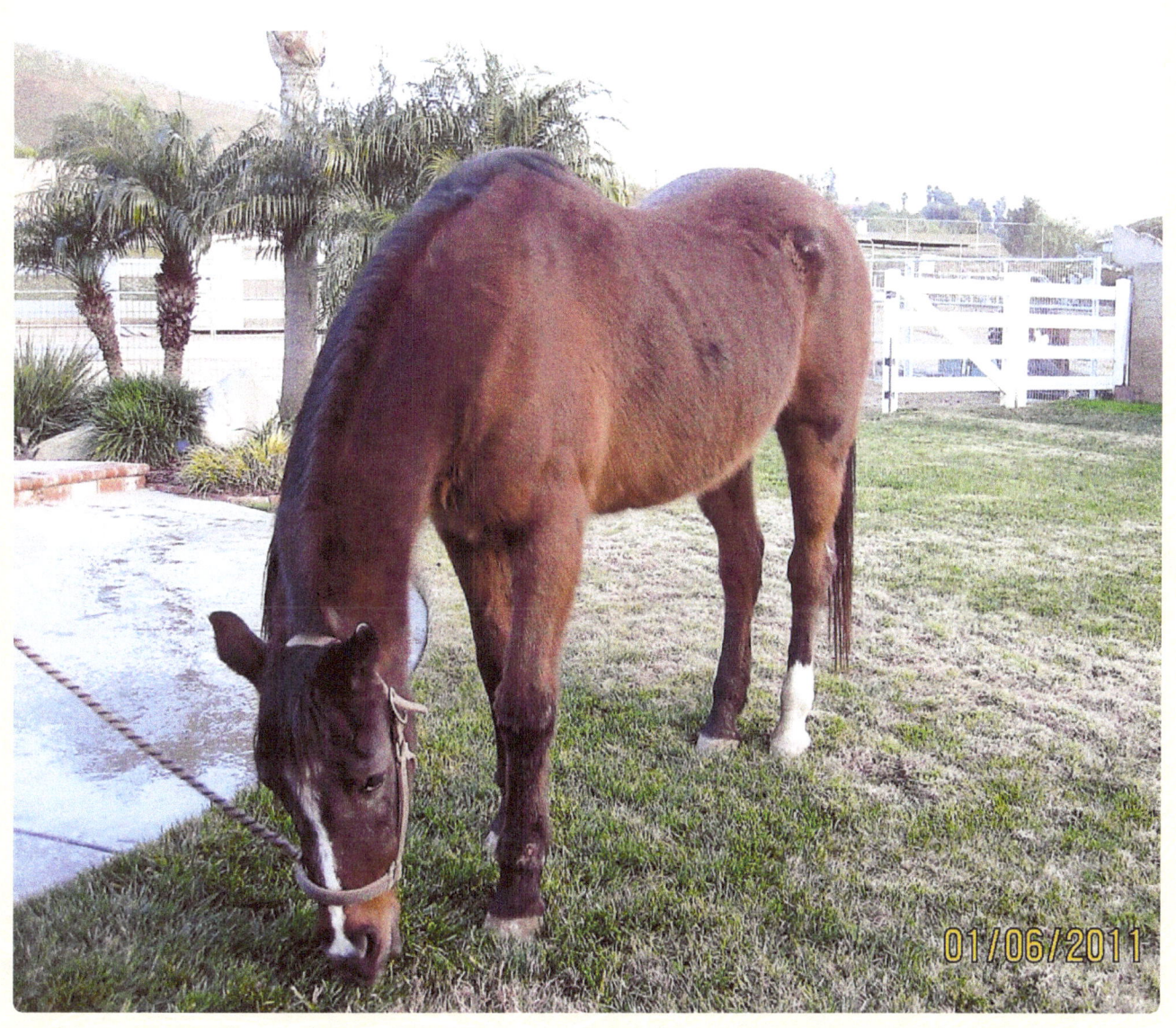

Wings at 32

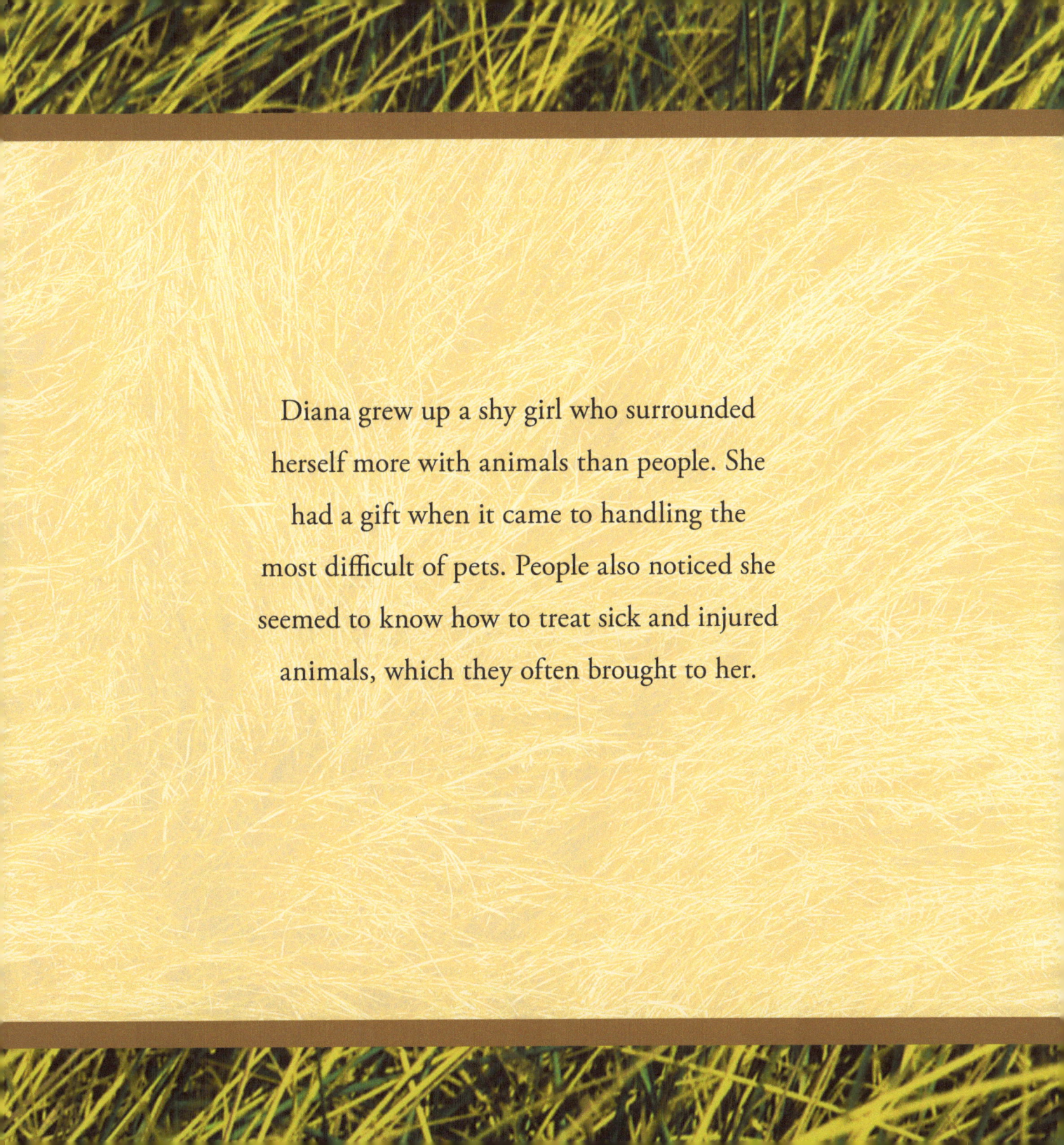

Diana grew up a shy girl who surrounded herself more with animals than people. She had a gift when it came to handling the most difficult of pets. People also noticed she seemed to know how to treat sick and injured animals, which they often brought to her.

www.ingramcontent.com/pod-product-compliance
Lightning Source LLC
Chambersburg PA
CBHW060810290526
45792CB00005BA/1592